ADVANCED

Jesus Shall Reign

Hymn Settings for Piano

Arranged by
Victor Labenske

Contents

Be Still, My Soul 4

Fairest Lord Jesus 8

His Eye Is on the Sparrow 12

Jesus Shall Reign 16

Sweet Hour of Prayer
    with I Need Thee Every Hour 20

Swing Low, Sweet Chariot 25

Trust and Obey 28

What a Friend We Have in Jesus 32

When the Roll Is Called Up Yonder 36

What Child Is This 42

Texts of the Hymns Arranged in *Jesus Shall Reign*

Be Still, My Soul
(page 4)

Be still, my soul: the Lord is on thy side.
Bear patiently the cross of grief or pain.
Leave to thy God to order and provide;
In every change, He faithful will remain.
Be still, my soul: thy best, thy heavenly Friend
Through thorny ways leads to a joyful end.

Be still, my soul: thy God doth undertake
To guide the future, as He has the past.
Thy hope, thy confidence let nothing shake;
All now mysterious shall be bright at last.
Be still, my soul: the waves and winds still know
His voice who ruled them while He dwelt below.

Be still, my soul: the hour is hastening on
When we shall be forever with the Lord.
When disappointment, grief and fear are gone,
Sorrow forgot, love's purest joys restored.
Be still, my soul: when change and tears are past
All safe and blessed we shall meet at last.

–Katharina von Schlegel; tr. by Jane L. Borthwick

Fairest Lord Jesus
(page 8)

Fairest Lord Jesus, Ruler of all nature,
O Thou of God and man the Son,
Thee will I cherish, Thee will I honor,
Thou, my soul's glory, joy and crown.

Fair are the meadows, fairer still the woodlands,
Robed in the blooming garb of spring;
Jesus is fairer, Jesus is purer
Who makes the woeful heart to sing.

Beautiful Savior! Lord of all the nations!
Son of God and Son of Man!
Glory and honor, praise, adoration,
Now and forevermore be Thine.

–Anonymous German Hymn

His Eye Is on the Sparrow
(page 12)

Why should I feel discouraged?
Why should the shadows come?
Why should my heart be lonely
And long for heaven and home
When Jesus is my portion? My constant friend is He.
His eye is on the sparrow, and I know He watches me;
His eye is on the sparrow, and I know He watches me.

"Let not your heart be troubled."
His tender words I hear,
And, resting on His goodness,
I lose my doubt and fear.

Though by the path He leadeth, but one step I may see,
His eye is on the sparrow, and I know He watches me.
His eye is on the sparrow, and I know He watches me.

Refrain

I sing because I'm happy,
I sing because I'm free,
For His eye is on the sparrow,
And I know He watches me.

–Civilla D. Martin

Jesus Shall Reign
(page 16)

Jesus shall reign where'er the sun
Does his successive journeys run;
His kingdom spread from shore to shore,
Till moons shall wax and wane no more.

People and realms of every tongue
Dwell on His love with sweetest song;
And infant voices shall proclaim
Their early blessings on His name.

Let every creature rise and bring
His grateful honors to our King;
Angels descend with songs again,
And earth repeat the loud "Amen!"

–Isaac Watts

Sweet Hour of Prayer
(page 20)

Sweet hour of prayer! sweet hour of prayer!
That calls me from a world of care,
And bids me at my Father's throne
Make all my wants and wishes known.
In seasons of distress and grief,
My soul has often found relief,
And oft escaped the tempter's snare
By thy return, sweet hour of prayer!

–William B. Walford

I Need Thee Every Hour
(page 23)

I need Thee every hour, in joy or pain;
Come quickly and abide, or life is in vain.

Refrain

I need Thee, O I need Thee;
Every hour I need Thee.
O bless me now, my Savior;
I come to Thee.

–Annie S. Hawks

Swing Low, Sweet Chariot
(page 25)

Refrain
Swing low, sweet chariot,
Coming for to carry me home,
Swing low, sweet chariot,
Coming for to carry me home.

I looked over Jordan, and what did I see?
Coming for to carry me home,
A band of angels coming after me,
Coming for to carry me home.

If you get there before I do,
Coming for to carry me home,
Tell all my friends I'm coming, too.
Coming for to carry me home.

–Traditional Spiritual

Trust and Obey
(page 28)

When we walk with the Lord in the light of His Word,
What a glory He sheds on our way!
While we do His good will, He abides with us still,
And with all who will trust and obey.

Refrain
Trust and obey, for there's no other way
To be happy in Jesus, but to trust and obey.

Not a shadow can rise, not a cloud in the skies,
But His smile quickly drives it away;
Not a doubt or a fear, not a sigh or a tear
Can abide while we trust and obey.

Then in fellowship sweet we will sit at His feet,
Or we'll walk by His side in the way.
What He says we will do, where He sends we will go;
Never fear, only trust and obey.

–John H. Sammis

What a Friend We Have in Jesus
(page 32)

What a Friend we have in Jesus,
All our sins and griefs to bear!
What a privilege to carry
Everything to God in prayer!
Oh, what peace we often forfeit,
Oh, what needless pain we bear,
All because we do not carry
Everything to God in prayer.

Are we weak and heavy-laden,
Cumbered with a load of care?
Precious Savior, still our refuge,
Take it to the Lord in prayer.
Do thy friends despise, forsake thee?
Take it to the Lord in prayer!
In His arms He'll take and shield thee;
Thou wilt find a solace there.

–Joseph M. Scriven

When the Roll Is Called Up Yonder
(page 36)

When the trumpet of the Lord shall sound,
    and time shall be no more,
And the morning breaks, eternal, bright and fair;
When the saved of earth shall gather
    over on the other shore,
And the roll is called up yonder, I'll be there.

Refrain
When the roll is called up yonder,
When the roll is called up yonder,
When the roll is called up yonder,
When the roll is called up yonder I'll be there.

On that bright and cloudless morning
    when the dead in Christ shall rise,
And the glory of His resurrection share;
When His chosen ones shall gather
    to their home beyond the skies,
And the roll is called up yonder, I'll be there.

–James M. Black

What Child Is This
(page 42)

What Child is this who, laid to rest
On Mary's lap is sleeping?
Whom angels greet with anthems sweet,
While shepherds watch are keeping?

Refrain
This, this is Christ the King,
Whom shepherds guard and angels sing;
Haste, haste, to bring Him laud,
The Babe, the Son of Mary.

Why lies He in such mean estate,
Where ox and ass are feeding?
Good Christians, fear, for sinners here
The silent Word is pleading.

So bring Him incense, gold and myrrh;
Come peasant, king to own Him.
The King of Kings salvation brings;
Let loving hearts enthrone Him.

–William C. Dix

Be Still, My Soul

Jean Sibelius
Arranged by Victor Labenske

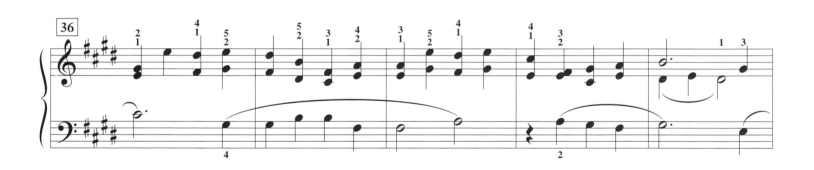

"Be still my soul, thy God doth undertake..."

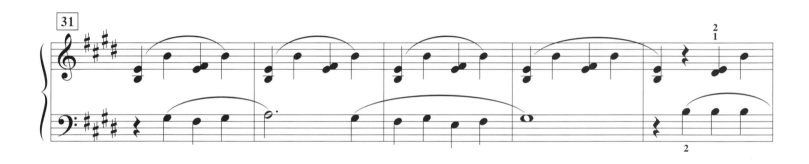

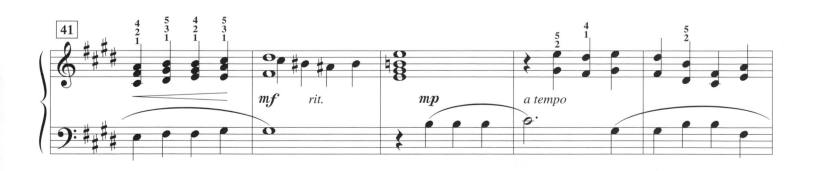

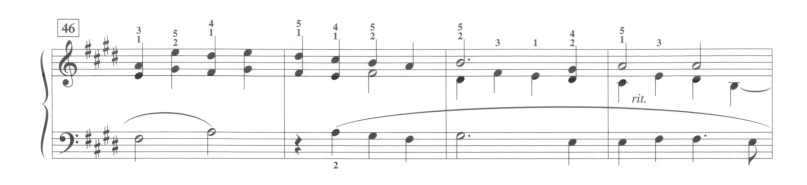

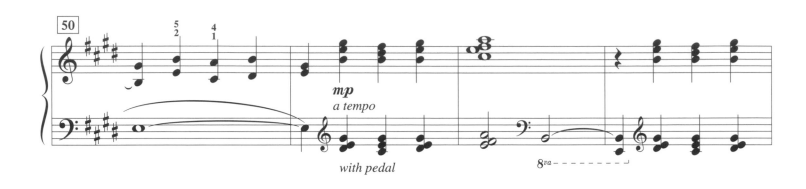

More broadly ($\flat$ = 56)

"Be still my soul, the hour is hastening on..."

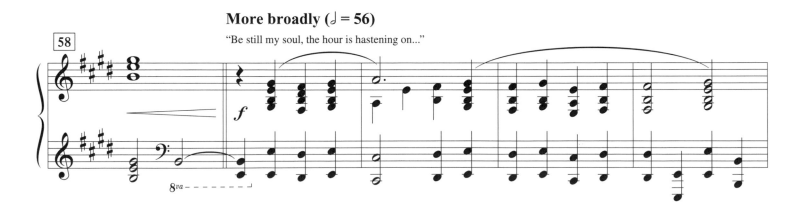

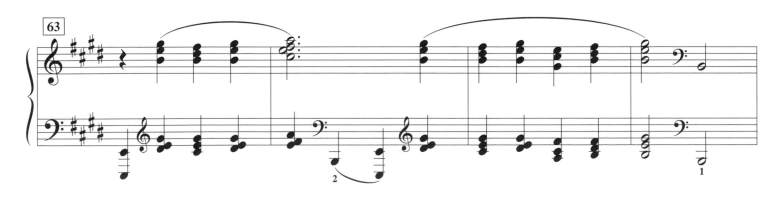

Fairest Lord Jesus

Anonymous, from
Schlesische Volkslieder, 1842

"Fairest Lord Jesus..."

with pedal

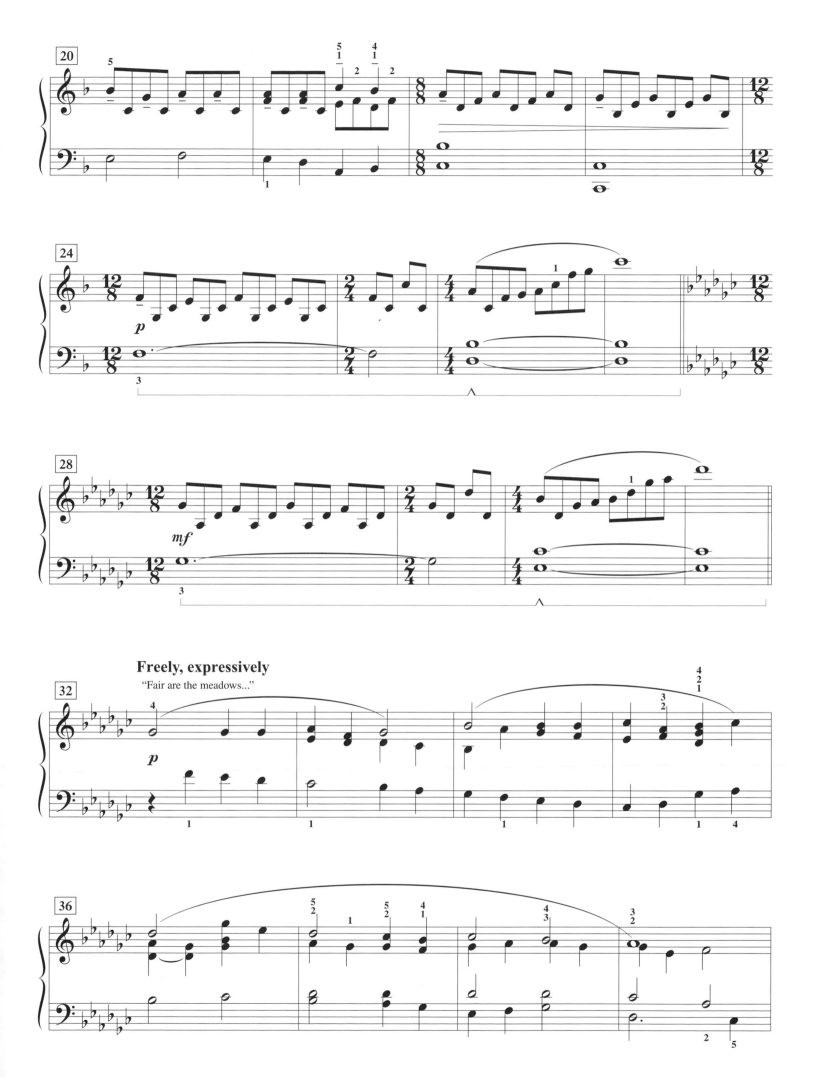

Freely, expressively

"Fair are the meadows..."

10

His Eye Is on the Sparrow

Charles H. Gabriel

In a vocal style (♩. = 69)

mp

with pedal

"Why should I feel discouraged..."

rit. *a tempo*

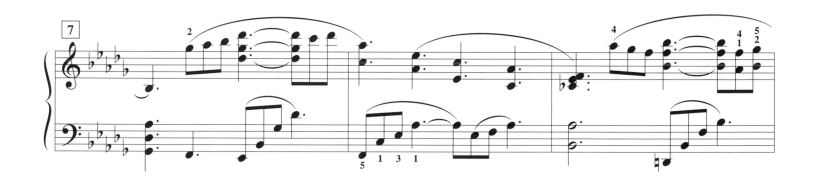

"Let not your heart be troubled..."

Jesus Shall Reign

John Hatton

("People and realms...")

mp

Sweet Hour of Prayer

with

I Need Thee Every Hour

William B. Bradbury

Meditatively (♩ = 60)

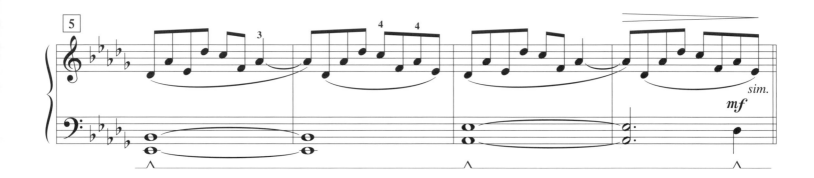

"Sweet hour of prayer...that calls me..."

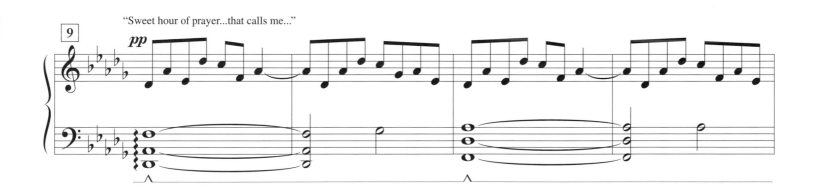

Slower (♩ = 52)
"I Need Thee Every Hour" (Robert Lowry)
"I need Thee every hour, in joy or pain..."

Swing Low, Sweet Chariot

Traditional Spiritual

Trust and Obey

Daniel B. Towner

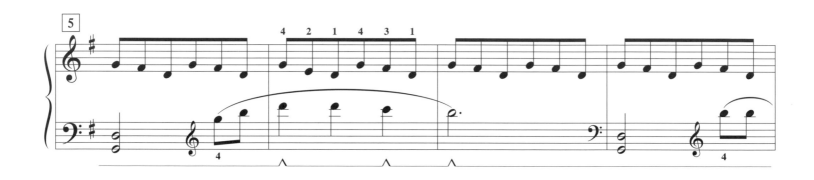

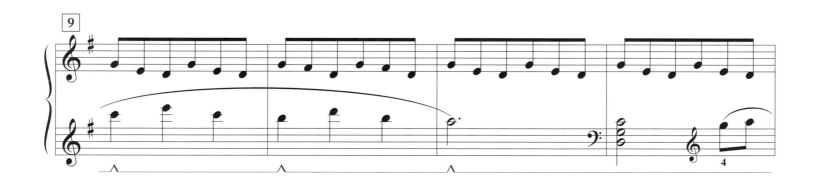

"Not a shadow can rise..."

"Then in fellowship sweet..."

What a Friend We Have in Jesus

Charles C. Converse

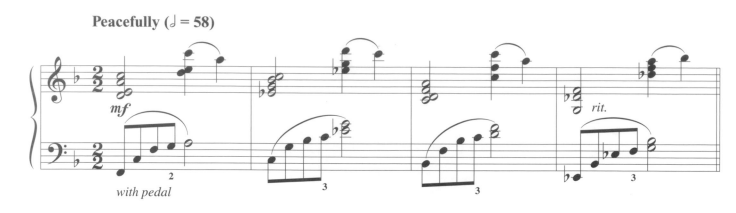

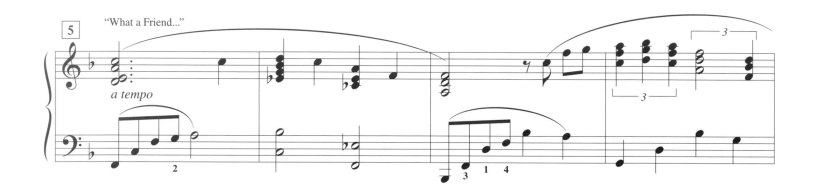

"Are we weak and heavy-laden..."

When the Roll Is Called Up Yonder

James M. Black

With energy (♩ = 96)

mf

with pedal

"When the trumpet..."

"On that bright and cloudless morning..."

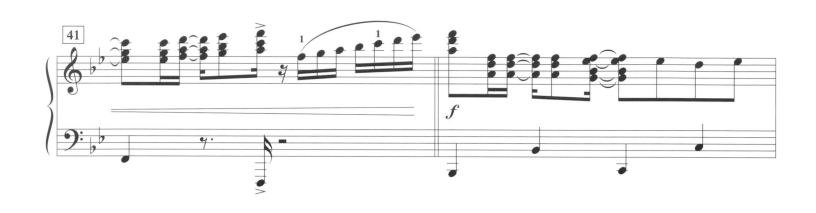

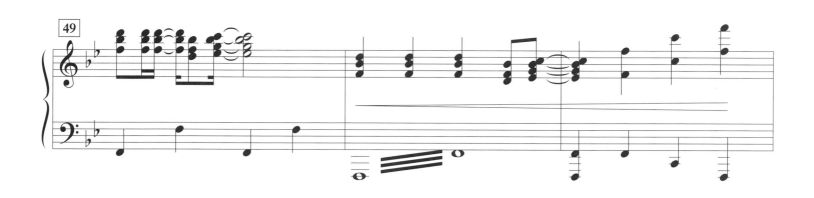

What Child Is This

Traditional English Melody

With wonder (♩. = 66)

44

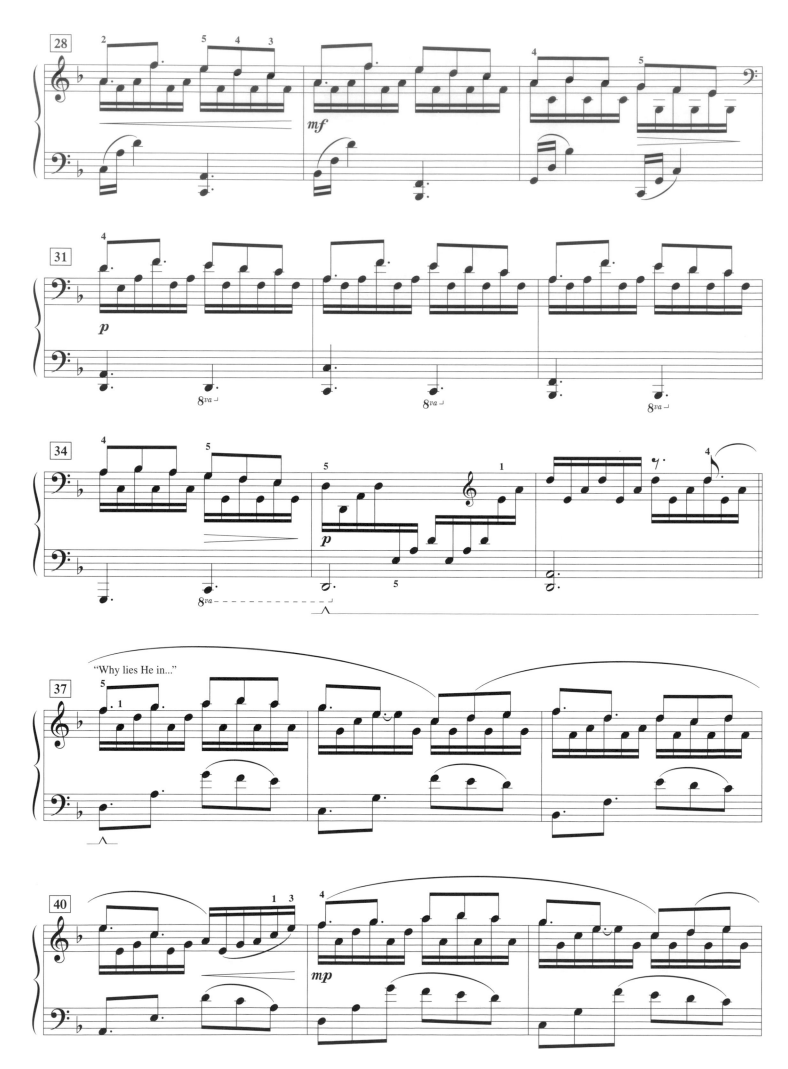

"So bring Him incense..."

ped. simile